D1557156

How to Make Sandwiches and Box Lunches

Gloria Goddard

Fredonia Books
Amsterdam, The Netherlands

How to Make Sandwiches and Box Lunches

by
Gloria Goddard

ISBN: 1-4101-0931-3

Creative Cookbooks
An Imprint of Fredonia Books
Monterey, California
http://www.creativecookbooks.com

CONTENTS

HOW TO MAKE SANDWICHES AND BOX LUNCHES

I

WHY SANDWICHES?

Not long ago, a one-time famous caterer wrote his memoirs. Somewhere within the pages of his very interesting book, he deplored the fact that Americans have lost the art of eating. We have become a race of sandwich eaters, he mourned. There is a great deal of truth in his indictment. The sandwich has become the main diet of at least seventy-five per cent of the working people of the country, and it has crept into home life too. Hot sandwiches are growing in favor as a dinner dish. Everywhere, in the cities, sandwich shops are springing up, wedged into two-by-four cubby-holes, where the food served is as constricted as the quarters. There is a lot to be said against this habit. On the other hand there is a lot to be said in favor of the sandwich. The trouble is not with the sandwich, but with the misuse of it. In its place, it is a most delightful bit of food; as a steady lunch diet, it is almost a crime.

What is the sandwich's place? It has many and various uses. Nor is the sandwich the simple thing it once was. In the forgotten past when an English nobleman invented it and gave his name to it, the sandwich was merely two slices of bread with a slice of meat between. The sandwich of today would scorn such humble ancestry. All sorts of amazing food contrivances bear the name of this once simple titbit. Sandwiches appear in startling shapes, in all manner of heights, rivaling the sky-scraper structures in some instances. So many and diverse are its forms that only imagination and the elasticity of word-meanings make it possible to call some of the things we see sandwiches.

The chief charm of sandwiches, in the eyes of the hostess, is the fact that, once prepared, there is no further fuss. They have only to be served, and eaten. No innumerable dishes to be passed and later washed. In the majority of cases, service plates are unnecessary. The sandwiches are passed and taken in the fingers. That is all. Nothing could be simpler. Small wonder, the average hostess regards this dish as a life-saver.

The guests should regard sandwiches in the same light. In the good old Victorian days. afternoon teas, card parties, evening affairs were all occasions of violent over-eating. Rich pastries, creamed chicken and lobster, Welsh rarebits, and the like were served about midnight. Afterwards the poor guests staggered to their homes, and indulged in nightmares. It would be interesting to gather the statistics of the decline of nightmares since the midnight supper passed out of existence. Sandwiches are the one sane thing to serve for parties of any kind.

This sounds like a monotonous proposal. It need not be. The different kinds of sandwiches are so numerous that it would take several books to explain them all. Just a little change makes a sandwich different. Perhaps the most commonly used filling for party sandwiches is cream cheese. With nuts, olives or pimentos it appears at every function, until everyone is tired of the thought of it. Cream cheese! Horrors! But try mixing it with anchovy paste and minced onions, or with minced water cress. No one will recognize the old familiar cream cheese. The varieties are endless.

Sandwiches can be served in a novel way at luncheons. Not the usual soggy gravy-soaked bread with a slab of meat, but unusual, fascinating affairs in which no bread appears at all. Oh, yes, you can make a sandwich without bread. Such delicacies will tempt the most bored guest. Sandwiches are ideal for bridge parties, since there need be no fuss in serving them. Dainty, unusual varieties add zest to the evening function. The picnic has always been the sandwich's playground, and for school or office lunches they are almost essential. So many occasions for serving them, and so few known ways of making these delicacies. Our aim is to bring to the attention of the hostess or the housewife newer, fresher ways of making these old stand-bys.

There are a few essential rules to remember. The first and perhaps the most important thing is the bread. Almost invariably, sandwiches are better and more tasty when made with any other bread than white bread. Rye, gluten, whole wheat, brown bread, nut bread, all make better sandwiches and give the most common varieties a touch of difference. Bread for sandwiches should never be fresh. Fresh bread is either too crumby or too soft to cut well. Buy bread at least one day old, or purchase it the day before you are going to use it and let it dry out. Never use toast for sandwiches that are not to be served immediately. Fresh crisp lettuce will keep for several hours in a sandwich, but if it stands too long it will become limp and tough.

A very sharp knife is essential. A smooth-edged knife, rather than the customary saw-edged bread knife is preferable. The latter is apt to make the bread crumby. It saves time and gives greater uniformity to cut the crust from the whole loaf before slicing. The butter for spreading should always be soft, but not melted. Allow the butter to stand in a warm place for at least half an hour before using, then beat it to a cream with a fork. If the butter is creamy it will not tear the bread and will spread more evenly.

Sandwiches for parties may be made hours before serving, and if kept right, be fresh when used. There are two ways of keeping them. Use large pieces of waxed paper. Spread one or two sheets on a plate. Pile the sandwiches on this and cover well, using one or two more pieces of the paper over the top. Be sure the sandwiches are completely covered. Then place in the ice box until ready to serve. Another way is to wring out a towel or napkin in cold water. Wring all the water out, leaving the towel as nearly dry as possible. Wrap the sandwiches in this and place in the ice box.

Sandwiches will keep for several days in this manner, providing the fillings are not easily perishable. The important thing is to keep the sandwiches away from the air, which dries them.

If sandwiches are to be picked up and eaten in the fingers, do not use bulky, slippery, or too creamy fillings. For instance, do not try to pass around club sandwiches for your guests to pick up and eat. It will prove disastrous to your rugs.

On the other hand, sandwiches without tops, the so-called canapés, may be served to be eaten in the fingers, provided the filling remains firm. These sandwiches, if artfully made and arranged, make a table or tray look very beautiful.

II

SAVORY BUTTERS

Here is one of the sandwich secrets that few people know about, or if they do know, ignore. The simplest of sandwiches can be improved by the use of a savory butter. These butters can be prepared and kept as indefinitely as plain butter. Almost any of these butters can be used without any additional filling for sandwiches for afternoon teas, or at any time when a light, tasty sandwich is required.

The following recipes are all based on one-half pound of butter.

Water Cress Butter—Beat the butter until very creamy. Add one-half tablespoonful of lemon juice and one-half cupful of minced water cress. Blend thoroughly. Keep in a cool place, and beat to a creamy consistency before using. Parsley, mint or chicory may be substituted for water cress with equally good results.

Lemon Butter—Add two tablespoonfuls of lemon juice and the grated rind of one-quarter lemon to the butter. Orange may be used for a sweet butter.

Onion Butter—Add to the butter, one medium-sized onion, minced and one tablespoonful of hot butter. Chives or scallions may be used. It is better to use Spanish onions in all sandwich fillings or butters because they have not the strong lingering odor and taste of ordinary onions. One-third of a Spanish onion would be sufficient to make onion butter.

Pimento Butter—Pound one-quarter cupful of minced pimento with one teaspoonful of lemon juice, and add to the butter. Ripe olives may be substituted, in which case use one teaspoonful of olive oil in place of the lemon juice.

Fish Butters—Use any of the fish pastes, such as anchovy, sardine, or lobster. To the butter add one-half cupful of a fish paste and three tablespoonfuls of lemon juice. The fish meats may be used, but this is more trouble because they must be pounded to a paste first.

One very delightful butter is made with one-third cupful of sardines, an equal amount of smoked salmon. The sardines must be skinned and boned then pounded together with the salmon. Add the lemon juice to the fish before pounding, as this will facilitate the process. Then add to the butter.

Devil Butter—Mix four tablespoonfuls of dry mustard with an equal amount of Worcestershire sauce, a dash of cayenne and one-quarter teaspoonful of salt. Add this to the butter.

Curry Butter—Add two tablespoonfuls of curry powder to the butter.

Lemon or onion butter is excellent for any fish sandwiches. The onion or the devil butter goes well with cold meats. The curry butter is splendid for cold chicken or turkey. Use the pimento, olive or water cress butters for anchovy, sardine or cheese sandwiches.

III

HOT SANDWICHES

If you are going to serve the usual hot roast meat sandwiches it is best to use toast. No recipe for these will be given because everyone knows how to fix them, and they are neither interesting nor particularly delectable dishes. The hot sandwiches suggested below are only the more unusual ones.

Ham and Egg—Toast one side of moderately thick slices of bread, using twice as many slices as persons to be served. For eight slices of bread beat two eggs with two tablespoonfuls of milk. Season with salt and pepper. Place in a frying pan with one tablespoonful of melted butter and cook until creamy. Stir constantly to keep even. When thick enough so that the mixture will not run, remove from fire. Place the toast, toasted side down, on a flat pan. Spread half of the slices with the egg mixture. Butter the untoasted side of the other four slices and cover with grated cheese. Place under a grill and toast until the eggs become firm and the cheese melted. While the toast is cooking, broil four slices of ham. Have the slices the same size as the bread, and not too thick. When cooked, place the egg-filled slice of toast on a plate, lay the broiled ham on top, and cover with the cheese-filled toast.

Chicken Liver—Use mashed potatoes, instead of bread, as a base. Form the potato into cakes about half an inch thick and three or four inches square. Make two cakes for every person. Cover the bottom of a frying pan with half an inch of olive oil. Heat to boiling point. Lay the cakes in the hot oil. Cook very quickly and with a cake turner. When a rich brown on both sides remove to brown paper and let drain for two minutes. Have the chicken livers prepared before fixing the potatoes: One-half pound of chicken livers will serve four people. Wash, remove the membrane and cut into small pieces. Drop into a frying pan covered with hot butter or hot olive oil. Cook until a deep brown. When done, remove the livers. Add to the oil in the pan one-quarter cupful of finely chopped mushrooms, one tablespoonful of minced onion and an equal amount of parsley. Let the mushrooms brown slightly. Cream two tablespoonfuls of flour with half as much butter. Pour over the mixture in the pan two cupfuls of milk. When heated add the flour and stir until thickened. Add one tablespoonful of lemon juice and salt and pepper to taste. Spread the potato cakes with devil butter, and place the livers on one cake. Top with the other cake, and pour the sauce over the top.

Sweet Potato and Chestnuts—Make sweet potato cakes in the same manner as white potato cakes, preparing two for each serving. Shell and blanch one-half pound of chestnuts to serve four persons. Boil the chestnuts in very little water until tender. Mash or press through a sieve. Add enough milk or cream to form a fairly thick purée. Place in a saucepan and put over a low fire. Add one tablespoonful of lemon juice, salt and pepper to taste, two tablespoonfuls of butter. Cook until thoroughly heated. Spread the potato cakes with parsley butter. Place one cake on each plate. Fill with some of the chestnut mixture, and cover with a second cake.

Chicken and Egg Plant—Peel and slice the egg plant into half inch slices. Use only the large center slices, allowing two slices for each person. Fry in deep fat. To serve four persons, heat in a very little stock or milk two cupfuls of diced chicken meat, one finely chopped small onion, one sprig of parsley, minced. When heated, place one slice of egg plant on each plate, cover with some of the chicken, and top with another slice of egg plant. Pour over the top Hollandaise sauce or any rich cream sauce. Turkey, duck, crab meat, shrimps or lobster may be used in place of the chicken. If a cream sauce is used, the egg plant should be spread with curry butter.

Creamed Duck—This is a good way to use left-over duck or goose. To serve four persons make three cupfuls of fairly thick cream sauce. Add to this two cupfuls of diced duck meat, one minced onion, a bit of minced parsley and salt and pepper to taste. As a base use rice fritters. To every two cupfuls of cold cooked rice add one beaten egg. Season and fry in deep hot fat. Make the cakes large and thin. Butter with apple butter (the ordinary commercial variety) and place one fritter on each plate. Cover with some of the creamed duck, and top with a second fritter.

Curry Sandwiches—Make as above, using any left-over fowl or fish. Use curry butter instead of apple butter.

Bread Baskets—This is an excellent way to serve any creamed meat or fish sandwich. Cut two inch slices from white or whole wheat bread. With a very sharp knife, remove the crust. Cut out the center of each slice leaving a one-half inch rim and bottom. Dip the cups into melted butter, being sure that every part is covered with butter. Place on a pan and bake in a very hot oven for about five minutes, or until the bread baskets are a golden brown. Fill with any creamed filling. Creamed mushrooms, creamed fowl, creamed crab flakes make excellent fillings. Scatter Parmesan cheese over the tops and place under a hot grill until the top surface browns. This makes a delightful luncheon dish, or if filled with a light filling, a beautiful bridge party dish.

IV

TEAS AND BRIDGE PARTIES

The one major thing to remember when preparing refreshments for any afternoon affair is that the dishes served must be light and tempting. Your guests have had luncheon before arriving at your home, and are presumably going home for dinner. It is therefore unnecessary to serve them a full meal. Make your sandwiches very dainty, with light appetizing fillings. Canapés are almost the best type of sandwich to serve on these occasions.

CANAPES

Caviare—Slice whole wheat bread into half-inch slices. Cut into fancy shapes with cooky cutters. Dip into melted butter and fry quickly. Slice hard-cooked eggs and remove the yolk from each slice. Place a ring of the egg white on each piece of bread. Empty the caviare into a bowl and sprinkle with lemon juice. Add one teaspoonful of minced onion for each two tablespoonfuls of caviare. Mix thoroughly and arrange some of the mixture in the center of each egg ring. Press the egg yolk through a sieve and decorate each canapé with it. Three eggs and one small can of caviare will make approximately ten canapés.

Anchovy—Spread rounds of rye bread with anchovy butter and garnish the tops with mixed ripe olives and chives chopped very fine. Any of the other fish butters may be used in place of the anchovy.

Apple—Mix together one-half cupful of chopped apple, one-half cupful of thinly sliced celery, one-quarter cupful of chopped cooked beet, one tablespoonful of minced chili pepper, one teaspoonful of onion juice, three tablespoonfuls of French dressing, and one-quarter teaspoonful of salt. When these ingredients are well mixed, spread on small squares of toast buttered with lemon butter. Serve at once.

Sliced Apple—Use ripe red apples and do not

peel. Cut rings of apple about one-eighth inch thick. Remove the seed center. Cut bread rounds the same size as the apple rounds Spread the bread with water cress butter. Lay an apple round on each bread round. For every six canapes, mix together two tablespoonfuls of mayonnaise and one-quarter cupful of crumbled Roquefort cheese. When thoroughly blended, spread on the apple and serve.

Savory Caviare—Use thinly sliced rye bread cut in rounds or any fancy shape. Cream one-quarter cupful of butter. Add one tablespoonful each of minced capers, minced ripe olives and minced parsley, one tablespoonful of lemon juice and a dash of cayenne. For a better flavor, rub the bowl with a split garlic clove before creaming the butter. When the ingredients are well blended spread on the bread. Place one teaspoonful of caviare in the center of each canapé.

Pimento Cheese—Prepare six oblongs of toast. Grate one cupful of cheese and fill six canned pimentos with it. Lay one pimento on each slice of toast. Sprinkle with salt and place in a hot oven until the cheese is melted, or about eight minutes. Serve hot. These canapés must be served with forks.

Montauk—Prepare long thin strips of bread. Beat one egg. Mix into the egg one "snappy" cheese, one tablespoonful of milk, one-eighth teaspoonful of dry mustard, salt and pepper to taste. Blend to a smooth paste and spread on the bread strips. Lay a slice of bacon on each and broil about three minutes. Serve hot.

Salmon Cornucopias—Slice white bread very

thin, having removed the crust. Lay between damp towels for five minutes. Remove and place on a bread board. Cover each slice with a slice of very thin smoked salmon. The salmon should be slightly smaller than the bread. Roll into cornucopias. Press the outside edge down. If it will not stay in place, use a bit of butter to seal it. Fill with caviare and grated onion, using two tablespoonfuls of caviare and three of onion for every six cornucopias. Place a sprig of parsley in the top of each canapé.

Nut Cornucopias—Prepare the bread in the same way as above. When moistened spread with watercress butter. The butter must be very soft so as not to tear the bread. Roll into cornucopias and fill with finely chopped salted nuts which have been mixed with a very little mayonnaise.

There are any number of delightful combinations which can be served in the cornucopia. Fresh cucumbers make delicious fillings. In this case use onion butter as a spread. Watercress butter and finely chopped peeled radishes is a refreshing variation. Minced well-drained grapefruit with ripe olive butter is a unique combination. For a sweet cornucopia, spread the bread with parsley butter. Make a paste of very ripe bananas and lemon juice, using a scant teaspoonful for each large banana. Fill the cornucopias and garnish the top with a thin slice of candied lemon peel.

SANDWICHES

Miami—Use nut bread or brown bread. Melt

one tablespoonful of butter in a saucepan. Add one cupful of grated cheese, one teaspoonful of dry mustard, one-half tablespoonful of Worcestershire sauce and a dash of cayenne pepper. Stir over a slow fire until the cheese is melted and the mixture smooth. Beat two egg yolks with one cupful of thin cream or rich milk. Add the cheese mixture and beat thoroughly. Cook in a double boiler for two mirutes. Cool and spread on the bread. Top with another slice of bread. Cut in thin strips and serve.

Cuban Folds—Beat three small cream cheeses into one-quarter cupful of cream. When the mixture is smooth add one cupful of finely chopped walnuts and one cupful of chopped pineapple. The pineapple may be fresh or canned. If canned, drain very dry before chopping. Mix all together and fill between thin slices of brown bread previously buttered with lemon butter.

Olivettes—Mash one cupful of Roquefort cheese until smooth and season with a dash of cayenne and a few drops of Worcestershire sauce. Add one-half cupful of chopped ripe olives, and moisten mixture with enough mayonnaise to make it spread easily. Spread brown bread with peanut butter, then with the above mixture. Cover with brown bread buttered with peanut butter and cut in very small squares.

Favorites—Use rye bread sliced very thin. Cream together two tablespoonfuls of butter and one-half cupful of grated American cheese. Add two tablespoonfuls of anchovy paste, one-fourth teaspoonful each of paprika and dry mustard and one-half cupful of finely chopped ripe olives. Mix well and fill between slices of the bread.

Tomato and Horse-radish—Use rye bread, and very firm tomatoes. Peel the tomatoes and place on ice until thoroughly chilled. Mix one-quarter cupful of mayonnaise with an equal amount of drained horse-radish. Spread the bread with this mixture. Lay very thin slices of tomato between the bread. Cut sandwiches into strips and serve. These cannot stand too long, as the tomato will make the bread soggy.

Nasturtium—These are delightful and, if you have a garden, very cheap. Use the petals or the leaves of nasturtiums. Wash, drain and chill. Spread thin slices of whole wheat bread with mayonnaise and fill with the nasturtium. It gives a pretty color note to fill some of the sandwiches with the leaves, others with the petals.

Caviare Rolls—Rolled sandwiches are easy to make, if proper care is taken, and are a charming addition to any sandwich plate. Remove the crust from a day-old sandwich loaf. With a very sharp knife slice the bread lengthwise so that you have quarter-inch thick strips the full length of the bread. Lay these strips between dampened napkins and set aside for ten minutes. Lay the moistened strips of bread on a bread board. Spread with onion butter that is very soft. Then spread with caviare paste. Start with the narrow end nearest you and roll away from you pressing lightly as you roll. Roll slowly and carefully so as not to break the bread. When the entire length is rolled up, press the end against the side of the roll. Wrap tightly in a moist napkin and set aside for half an hour. Unwrap and with a sharp knife slice the roll into half inch slices.

Any smooth filling may be used for this type of sandwich. Cream cheese with pimento gives the effect of a jelly roll. Water cress, chicory, or parsley butter alone make beautiful rolled sandwiches.

Marble Rolls—For these sandwiches use sandwich bread and whole wheat or gluten bread. Cut the long strips as thin as possible, less than one-quarter of an inch. Cut even lengths of white and whole wheat bread and moisten as above. Lay the white strip on the bread board and butter with lemon butter and sardine paste. Lay the whole wheat bread on top of the white bread. Butter with chicory butter. Roll in the same manner as above, and wrap in a moist napkin. Cut in half inch slices when ready to serve as stated in above recipe.

Celery Sandwiches—Add to two cups of minced celery one tablespoonful each of apples, nuts, and ripe olives, all minced. Mix with enough mayonnaise to make an easy spreading paste. Slice Boston brown bread in thin slices and butter, and fill the celery filling between two slices. Cut each sandwich in half, making half-moon patterns.

Cucumber—Use rye bread. Slice the cucumbers very thin and marinate in lemon juice for half an hour. Spread the bread with onion butter and sour cream dressing. Lay slices of the cucumber over this and top with a second slice of bread. (See Chapter VII for dressings.)

Water Cress—Use rye bread. Mix three small cream cheeses with enough mayonnaise to make an easily spread paste. Run a bunch of water cress through a food chopper and mix with the cheese. Spread the rye bread with butter and fill with the water cress paste. Cut in thin finger strips.

Mock Crab—Use white, whole wheat or gluten bread. Cut thin slices and spread with pimento butter. Cream two tablespoonfuls of butter, add one-quarter teaspoonful each of salt and dry mustard, and one teaspoonful each of lemon juice and anchovy paste, and one tablespoonful of chopped gherkins. Blend thoroughly and spread between slices of bread. Cut in small squares.

Nut Dreams—Add to one cupful of finely chopped nuts enough sour cream dressing to make a smooth paste. Butter thin slices of Boston brown bread and fill with the nut mixture. Cut in half-moons.

Tartare—Separate endive leaves and marinate in French dressing for ten minutes. Cut strips of whole wheat bread the shape and length of the endive leaves. Spread with Tartare sauce. Lay one leaf between each two strips of bread.

Date—These are the nicest sweet sandwiches. Chop fine one-half cup of dates and an equal amount of English walnut meats, and mix with one-half cupful of cream. Cut whole wheat bread into rounds. Spread with orange butter and fill with the date mixture. Boston brown bread may be used, if preferred. A dainty touch is the addition of a half walnut on top of each sandwich.

Roquefort Cheese—Spread thin slices of rye bread with onion butter. Mix one-half cupful of sour cream dressing with one-quarter pound of Roquefort cheese. Blend to a smooth paste. Season with a dash of cayenne. Add one-quarter cupful of minced water cress. Spread between slices of the bread and cut in fancy shapes.

Ribbons—Cut an equal number of thin slices of white and whole wheat bread. Spread a white slice with parsley butter. Cover with a brown slice and spread with pimento butter. Alternate until there are three of each kind. Do not spread the last slice. Cut the layers into half-inch slices.

All white bread may be used, or all whole wheat, and any variety of fillings. Be sure to choose fillings of different colors to get the right effect.

V

EVENING AFFAIRS

In choosing sandwiches for evening parties you have a much wider selection than when picking them for the afternoon affairs. All of the sandwiches suggested for the afternoon refreshments may be used for evening parties, and a large assortment besides. In general, evening refreshments are not served until after ten-thirty, sometimes not until midnight. There is to be no meal afterward, so the guests have a keener appetite for dainty food. There is a pleasing variety of meat and fish sandwiches that may be served at such times. Even then, it is not wise to have to much heavy food. Serve one or two kinds of meat or fish sandwiches, and one or two kinds of the lighter ones. At all times sandwiches must be dainty. The crust must always be removed from the bread, except in the case of nut bread and Boston brown bread, neither of which really have a crust. Sandwiches should be small. Cut them either in fancy shapes with a cooky cutter, or in small square or narrow strips.

CANAPES

Any of those suggested for bridge parties may be served. Have several kinds and arrange them on a large plate or platter. Avoid canapés requiring forks for eating them.

Chicken Curry—Cut the whole wheat bread into rounds slightly larger than a slice of cucumber. Cut as many thin slices of cucumber as there are rounds of bread. Marinate the cucumber in French dressing for fifteen minutes. Mix together one-half cupful of chopped cooked chicken, an equal amount of chopped cooked ham, two tablespoonfuls of butter, one tablespoonful of chutney, one-quarter teaspoonful of curry powder, an equal amount of salt and a dash of paprika. Pound to a paste. Spread on the bread rounds, and garnish with the sliced cucumber, placing one slice on each round.

Ham and Cucumber—Cut rye bread in long

thin fingers. Cut cucumbers lengthwise into thin slices slightly smaller than the bread. Marinate the cucumber in French dressing for fifteen minutes. Mix one cupful of minced cooked ham with enough sour cream dressing to make a smooth paste. Spread on the bread. Drain the cucumber and lay one slice on each canapé.

Ham—Use rye bread cut in any desired shape. Mix one cup of minced cooked ham, two teaspoonfuls of currant jelly, one-half teaspoonful of melted butter and a dash of paprika. Blend to a paste and spread on the bread. Mince one green pepper. Drain and mince one canned pimento. Garnish one-half of the canapés with the green pepper and the rest with the pimento.

SANDWICHES

Whitstable—Marinate a tightly packed cupful of broken shrimps for two hours in two tablespoonfuls of French dressing. Add one-half cupful of finely chopped lettuce and water cress and one-quarter cupful of chopped onions. Let stand for five minutes. Separate three hard-cooked eggs. Mash the yolks and add to the shrimp mixture. Chop the whites and add. Mix with a small amount of mayonnaise dressing and spread on whole wheat bread which has been previously spread with lemon butter. Top with a second slice of bread and cut into dainty shapes.

Chicken Liver—Use whole wheat bread. Boil one-half pound of chicken livers in very little water until done. Cool. Drain and mash. Add a small amount of the liquor and enough mayonnaise to make a smooth paste. Add two tablespoonfuls of minced onion and an equal amount of minced parsley, and seasoning to taste. Blend thoroughly and spread on bread buttered with devil butter.

Calf's Liver—Use rye bread. Boil half a pound of calf's liver until thoroughly cooked. Drain and press through a sieve. When cool add one-half cupful of minced olives, an equal amount of finely chopped crisp bacon, one teaspoonful of minced onions and enough mayonnaise to make a smooth paste. Add salt and cayenne, if necessary. Spread between slices of rye bread and cut in small squares. The olives may be omitted, or the bacon may be omitted.

Swiss Cheese—Butter rye bread with devil butter. Lay a thin slice of Swiss cheese on top of a slice of rye bread. Spread the second slice of bread with devil butter and with minced ham mixed with mayonnaise. Join the two slices and cut into strips.

Cucumber and Onion—Use rye bread. Mix equal amounts of diced cucumber and minced Spanish onion. Put in a shallow dish and cover with French dressing. Let stand in a cold place for one hour. Drain. Spread the butter with water cress butter and fill with the cucumber and onion filling.

Lobster—Use white or whole wheat bread. Fresh boiled or a good quality of canned lobster may be used. Cut the lobster in small pieces. For every two cupsful of lobster meat use one cupful of finely chopped celery and one teaspoonful of minced onion. Mix together with enough mayonnaise to spread easily. Spread the bread with parsley butter. Cut the bread into crosswise strips and lay one endive leaf on each strip. Fill with the lobster mixture and top with another strip of bread.

Olive and Nut—Use Boston brown bread or whole wheat bread. Mix equal parts of chopped nut meats (walnuts, pecans or cashews are best) and chopped ripe olives with enough mayonnaise to spread easily. Spread the bread with lemon butter, then fill with the nut mixture.

Or, spread the bread with curry butter.

Or, mix the nuts and olives with sour cream, or cottage cheese thinned with cream and spread the bread with devil butter. This last makes exceptionally good sandwiches.

Parker House Rolls—Bend back the top of the roll without breaking. With a sharp knife remove the soft center. Fill with minced chicken, minced ham, minced tongue. Press together, and heat until crisp. Serve when cool. These sandwiches must be prepared within an hour of serving as the rolls lose their crispness if allowed to stand too long.

Pâté de Foie Gras—This delicacy is largely ignored because most people do not know where to obtain it, and those who do believe it to be very expensive. It can be purchased by the pound in the best delicatessen stores or in cans almost anywhere. It is not expensive because it is so rich only a small quantity need be used. Rye bread is best for such sandwiches. If bought by the pound, have it sliced very thin. Spread the bread with onion butter or devil butter. Lay a slice of the pâté de foie gras on a slice of bread. Sprinkle with lemon juice and top, with another slice of bread. Cut into very thin strips for serving.

If canned pâté de foie gras is purchased, mix the paste with finely chopped onion and lemon juice. Spread on thin slices of bread previously buttered with devil butter. Cut into thin strips.

Smoked Salmon—Use rye bread. Spread the bread with lemon butter. Mince small pickled onions and spread on the bread. Lay a slice of smoked salmon on top and cover with a second slice of bread. Cut into small squares.

Shad Roe—Cook and cool the shad roe. Mash with enough mayonnaise to make a smooth paste. Spread whole wheat bread with lemon butter and minced water cress. Spread the alternate slices with lemon butter and the roe mixture. Put together and cut into strips. Any fish roe may be used instead of the shad roe. It is best to wrap the roe in a cloth and boil them.

Spinach—Thoroughly drain cooked spinach. Mince it and season with salt and pepper. To every cupful of the minced spinach add one-quarter cupful of anchovy paste and one table-spoonful of lemon juice. Blend thoroughly. Spread whole wheat or rye bread with onion butter and fill with the spinach. Cut in small squares.

Attractive ribbon sandwiches can be made by spreading white bread with lemon butter and anchovy paste. Top with whole wheat bread spread with onion butter and minced spinach. Repeat until there are three white slices and three whole wheat slices. Press firmly together and slice lengthwise into half-inch slices.

The mixed spinach and anchovy filling is a nice spread for rolled sandwiches also. White bread mst be used for these, as whole wheat bread is too crumbly to roll alone.

Egg Cornucopias—Spread white bread with plain butter then with deviled ham (canned). Fashion into cornucopias and fill first with finely chopped egg white mixed with celery. Fill the top with the egg yolk mixed with mayonnaise. Stick a sprig of parsley in the top of each.

Another good combination: Spread the bread with parsley butter. Make the cornucopias and fill with a mixture of equal parts of diced cooked beets and minced pickled onions and a small amount of mayonnaise dressing.

Tomato—Tomato sandwiches are refreshing, but must be made with care. They cannot be allowed to stand too long, as the tomato makes the bread soggy. One combination: Cut rye bread into rounds slightly larger than the tomato slices. Peel and chill firm ripe tomatoes. Slice into thin slices. Butter the bread with water cress butter. Lay a slice of tomato on top. Mix minced ripe olives with mayonnaise, using one tablespoonful of the olives for every three tablespoonfuls of the mayonnaise. Spread on top of the tomato. Top with a second round of bread.

Or, spread the bread with devil butter. Lay a slice of tomato on top. Cover with caviare mixed with an equal amount of minced onion. Top with a second round of bread.

Or spread the bread with sardine paste. Chop the tomato and strain slightly. Mix two table-spoonfuls of mayonnaise and one teaspoonful of minced onion and one-half cupful of chopped lettuce with every cupful of tomato. Spread on the bread and top with a second slice. These sandwiches may be cut in any desired shape.

Deviled Ham and Chicken—Spread whole wheat bread with plain butter then with deviled ham. Lay slices of chicken in French dressing for one-half hour. Drain and lay between slices of the bread. Cut in strips.

Bread Loaf—This is a beautiful dish to serve when the refreshments are to be eaten seated at a table. Remove the crust from a sandwich loaf. With a very sharp knife slice the bread lengthwise into quarter-inch slices. The bread should slice into at least six slices. Place the bottom one on a bread board. Spread with onion butter then with the spinach filling, omitting the anchovy paste. Place the second slice on top. Spread with cream cheese mixed with mayonnaise. Put another layer on top and spread with pimento butter and a paste made of mashed pimentoes and French dressing. Repeat until all the slices are used. Do not put a filling on the top layer. Press firmly together. Cover the sides and top with cream cheese thinned to spreading consistency with cream and colored with green or red vegetable coloring. Serve whole and slice at the table.

Other good combinations: onion butter and anchovy paste, Roquefort filling, nut filling. Or, deviled ham, minced chicken mixed with parsley, cream cheese and pimento.

The first combination gives the best color scheme. Ribbon sandwiches may be made this way, in which case, the cheese covering is omitted and the sandwiches sliced and served on a plate.

Banana—Sometimes a few sweet sandwiches are desirable. This recipe is a delicious one. Use whole wheat or Boston brown bread. The latter is best. Spread with orange butter. Mash ripe bananas to a smooth paste with one teaspoonful of lemon juice for each banana. Add a dash of cayenne pepper. Spread between slices of the bread. Cut in fancy shapes.

Sponge Cake—Slice loaf sponge cake into thin slices. Spread with lemon butter. Mix cream cheese with chopped walnut meats and a small amount of sour cream. Fill between slices of the cake. Cut in strips.

Dates and Cream Cheese—Use Boston brown bread. Mix one cupful of chopped dates with three small cream cheeses and enough mayonnaise to make an easy spread. Fill between slices of the bread, and cut in half-moons.

Orange and Cream Cheese—Use whole wheat or Boston brown bread. Peel and remove the fiber and seeds from one large orange. Cut into very small pieces. Mix with three small cream cheeses. If the mixture is too stiff to spread easily, thin with a small amount of cream. Spread the bread with the mixture and cut into small shapes.

Apple and Bacon—Use whole wheat bread. Spread the bread with lemon butter. Peel and remove the seeds from three ripe juicy apples.

Run through a food chopper. Add two table-spoonfuls of minced water cress and one cupful of finely chopped crisp bacon. Mix with a small amount of French dressing. Spread between slices of the bread and cut in small squares.

VI

LUNCH AND PICNIC SANDWICHES

Sandwiches for picnics and other box lunches must be of sturdier quality than fancy sandwiches for parties. In general such sandwiches are prepared to be the main part of the meal and must therefor contain a certain amount of actual food. When preparing sandwiches for box lunches, it is better to allow one good filling sandwich for each person than several light ones wherein the bread is the chief food. Too much bread is not good for anyone. Of course, any of the lighter sandwiches suggested in the foregoing chapters may be used as side delicacies, but it is best to use as few of these as possible.

In preparing sandwiches for box lunches, it is not necessary to remove the crusts, nor need they be cut in elaborate shapes. It is wiser to cut each sandwich in three sections so that it may be easily handled.

Tomatoes and lettuce should not be used in sandwiches that are going to be packed for any length of time. Wrap each sandwich separately in wax paper before packing. Never use toast for sandwiches that are to be packed. Endive may be used instead of lettuce, since it retains its crispness for a much longer time. In cutting rye bread, cut at a sharp angle to get a larger slice.

SANDWICHES

Cheese and Ham—Use rye bread. Spread the slices with onion butter. Lay a thin slice of Swiss cheese on a slice of bread and a slice of cold boiled ham on top. Spread the top ot the ham with Tartare sauce and top with a slice of rye bread.

Tongue, roast beef or corned beef or chicken may be substituted for the ham. Another delightful combination is ham and chicken and Swiss cheese. Tongue, chicken and Swiss cheese; roast beef, tongue or ham and Swiss cheese are also good. If using a combination of meats with Swiss cheese, deviled ham may be used instead of cold boiled ham. Spread the deviled ham over the onion butter on the bread and then fill with the other ingredients.

Combination Meat—Use rye or whole wheat bread. Spread with onion, water cress, chicory, devil or curry butter. Devil and curry butter are particularly good spreads for chicken and beef combinations. Lay a slice of chicken on a slice of bread. Spread with Tartare sauce, and cover with a slice of tongue or ham. Top with a second slice of bread.

Roast beef and chicken, roast beef and ham or tongue, corned beef and tongue or chicken make good combinations. If roast beef is used, a teaspoonful of horse-radish added to plain mayonnaise makes a more satisfactory dressing than Tartare sauce.

Mock Club—This is a delightful sandwich

for a box lunch, being almost a meal in itself. Use rye bread and remove the crusts. Spread with plain butter. On the first slice lay sliced chicken and cover thinly with Russian dressing. Place a slice of bread over this. Spread with Russian dressing and lay thin very crisp strips of bacon on top. Cover with another slice of bread. Lay a slice of tongue or corned beef on this and spread with Russian dressing. Top with a final slice of bread. The bacon will retain its crispness for hours, and the Russian dressing makes a fine substitute for tomatoes.

Liver Wurst—Combinations with liver wurst are appetizing and unusual. Use rye bread. Spread with devil butter. Remove the skin from thinly sliced liver wurst and lay slices on a piece of the bread. Top with a slice of Swiss cheese and a second slice of the bread.

Plain American cheese may be used with good result.

Liver wurst and ham or corned beef, or liver wurst and roast beef make nice combinations. If roast beef is used, butter the bread with devil or curry butter and spread a thin layer of horse-radish on the bottom slice. Cheese may be added to any of these combinations. Grated Parmesan cheese gives a new and unusual flavor.

Salami—This is an inexpensive and much ignored sandwich meat. Use rye bread. Spread the bread with lemon or onion butter. Remove the skin from thinly sliced salami and arrange the sl ces on a piece of bread. Cover with a very thin coating of prepared mustard and top with a slice of tongue and a final slice of bread.

Roast or corned beef may be substituted for the tongue. In this case, use a thin spread of horse-radish between the two meats.

Salami and Onion—Marinate the onion, which has been sliced in thin slices, in French dressing for fifteen minutes. Spread rye bread with devil butter. Cover a slice of the bread with salami, and top with onion slices and a second slice of bread. Spanish onions are the best for this purpose.

Ham and Egg—Mix one cupful of minced ham with one tablespoonful of minced ripe olives and an equal amount of minced pickled onions. Blend together with a very small amount of mayonnaise dressing. Spread whole wheat or rye bread with devil butter, then with some of the ham mixture. Cover with thin slices of hard-cooked egg and top with a second slice of bread.

Egg and Anchovy—Spread rye bread with lemon butter, then with anchovy paste. Lay thin slices of hard-cooked egg on top and cover with a second slice of bread. Sardine, lobster, caviare paste may be substituted for the anchovy paste. Or whole sardines or whole anchovies may be used.

Egg, Celery and Onion—Use whole wheat or rye bread. Hard-cook six eggs. Remove the yolks. Dice the whites and add one cupful of minced celery, and two tablespoonfuls of minced onion. Season to suit. Mash the egg yolks and add enough mayonnaise to make a thin paste. Spread the bread with parsley butter, then with the egg yolk paste. Fill with

the other mixture and top with a second slice
of bread.

Egg and Crab Meat—Use whole wheat or
white bread. Hard-cook three eggs. Separate
the yolks. Dice the whites and add to one cupful of shredded crab flakes. Add two tablespoonfuls of minced celery and a few capers.
Mix the mashed yolks with enough mayonnaise
to make a thin paste. Spread the bread with
devil butter and then with the mayonnaise.
Fill with the crab flakes and top with another
slice of bread.

Lobster flakes, finely cut shrimps, tuna fish
or canned salmon may be used instead of the
crab flakes.

Egg and Ripe Olives—Use whole wheat or
white bread. Spread the bread with pimento
butter. Mix one cupful of minced ripe olives
with enough mayonnaise to make a smooth
paste. Spread on the bread. Fill with slices
of hard-cooked egg.

Alligator Pear—Use rye or whole wheat
bread. Split and remove the skin from two
ripe alligator (avocada) pears. Cut in thin
slices and marinate in French dressing for
one-half hour. Spread the bread with water
cress butter. Cut two stalks of endive into
small pieces and spread over a slice of the
bread. Lay the drained slices of pear on top
of this and cover with a second slice of bread.

Alligator Pear and Meat—Use rye or whole
wheat bread. Prepare two ripe pears as above.
Drain and mash into a smooth pulp with a
small amount of the French dressing. Spread
the bread with devil butter, then with the pear

paste. Lay a slice of chicken, tongue, ham or roast beef on top and cover with bread.

Hearts of Palm—Use whole wheat or white bread. Spread the bread with onion butter, then with anchovy, or any fish paste. Drain the hearts of palm and slice into fairly thick slices. Place between two slices of bread. Hearts of palm may be purchased from any large grocery store or from any mail order house. They can be used in place of lettuce for any sandwich.

Salmon, Onion and Celery—Use rye bread. Spread the bread with lemon, devil or pimento butter. For every cupful of shredded canned salmon use one-half cupful of chopped celery and one tablespoonful of chopped pickled onions. Mix thoroughly with enough mayonnaise to make an easy spread. Fill between slices of the bread. Chopped endive may be added if desired.

Tuna Fish and Swiss Cheese—Use rye or whole wheat bread. Spread the bread with onion butter. Lay a thin slice of Swiss cheese on a slice of the bread. Add to every cupful of shredded Tuna fish one tablespoonful of finely chopped ripe olives. Moisten with mayonnaise and some of the liquor from the fish. Spread over the cheese and top with a slice of bread.

Calf's Liver, Bacon and Onion—Use whole wheat or rye bread. Spread the bread with water cress or chicory butter. Boil one-half pound of calf's liver until tender. Drain and cool. Slice into thin slices. Broil bacon until **very crisp.** Mince three small onions and marinate in French dressing for fifteen minutes. Season the liver with salt and pepper. Cover a slice of bread with slices of liver, top with crisp bacon, and sprinkle some of the onion on top. Cover with a second slice of bread.

Corned Beef and Cold Slaw—Prepare cold slaw with sour cream dressing. Use rye bread. Spread the bread with devil butter   Cover a slice of bread with thinly sliced corned beef. Spread the cold slaw on top and cover with a second slice of bread. Roast beef, ham or tongue may be used as a substitute for the corned beef.

Smoked Salmon and Cold Slaw—Use rye bread. Spread the bread with onion butter. Lay a slice of smoked salmon on a slice of bread. Sprinkle with lemon juice. Cover with cold slaw made with sour cream dressing and top with a slice of bread.

Hamburger Steak and Onion—Use whole wheat or rye bread. Spread the bread with devil butter. Form the hamburger steaks into very thin cakes about the same size as the slices of bread. Fry or broil quickly on a hot fire. When well browned and thoroughly done, remove from fire and cool. Slice Spanish onions and marinate in French dressing for fifteen minutes. Place a hamburger steak cake on a slice of bread, cover with onions and top with a second slice of bread.

Roast Beef and Horse-radish—Use whole wheat or rye bread. Spread the bread with devil, or onion butter. Lay a slice of roast beef on a slice of the bread and spread with a thin

layer of horse-radish. Top with another slice
of bread. Minced beef or potted beef may be
used instead of the roast beef.

Pickled Pig's Feet, Cold Slaw—Use rye bread.
Spread the bread with onion butter. Cut the
meat from the pig's feet and mince. Prepare
the cold slaw with French dressing. Spread
the meat on a slice of the bread and cover with
a thin layer of the cold slaw. Top with a
slice of bread.

Onion—These are delicious when served with
any of the meat sandwiches in which onion has
not been used, or they are very good alone.
Use rye bread. Spread the bread with any of
the fish butters, or with pimento butter and
cover each slice with endive leaves. Use only
Spanish onions. Peel and slice in thin slices.
Lay the onions in a dish and pour boiling water
over them. Allow to stand for one minute.
Drain and pour iced water over them. Stand
in a cold place for thirty minutes. The boiling
water removes the strong taste and makes the
onion more tender. The cold water restores
the crispness. When prepared, lay between
slices of the bread. Do not put anything on
the onion, even salt. Salt makes the onion
flabby.

Creamed Pork—Prepare Parker House rolls
as previously described. Use any left-over
cooked pork, or cold roast pork bought for the
purpose. Prepare Hollandaise sauce, and allow
it to cool. Add three cupfuls of the chopped
pork to the cool sauce, and fill the rolls. Left-
over chicken or ham or tongue may be used in

place of the pork. If ham is used, the sour cream dressing is better than the sauce.

Pork and Apple—This is another good use for left-over pork. Dice the pork, and the apples. Use ripe tart apples. Mix two cupfuls of pork, one cupful of apple, one tablespoonful of minced onion, an equal amount of minced celery and enough mayonnaise to make an easy spread. Spread whole wheat bread with parsley butter and fill with the mixture.

Tongue and Chestnuts—Use white or whole wheat bread. Spread with onion butter. Mash one-quarter pound of chestnuts which have been shelled and boiled until tender. Season with enough French dressing to make a smooth paste. Spread this on the bread. Lay slices of tongue over it, and top with a second slice of bread.

VII

A VARIETY OF DRESSINGS

One of the great contributing causes of monotony of sandwiches is the exclusive use of mayonnaise dressing. In the first place, the majority of people use too much of it, thus killing the flavor of the other ingredients. In the second place, no matter how varied the fillings may be, if every sandwich served contains mayonnaise, the whole lot has a similarity of taste. Often enough a dressing is not essential, provided a savory butter is used. French dressing is frequently better than mayonnaise. Certain substitutes are suggested below, which are more reasonable, in some cases, and in all cases, more varied.

DRESSINGS

Tartare Sauce—Mayonnaise is so easily obtainable these days that no one makes it, so no recipe will be given. Tartare sauce may also be purchased in most places, but, in the event that it is not obtainable, the following recipe is simple and delicious. Add to one cupful of mayonnaise one-quarter teaspoonful of dry mustard, two tablespoonfuls each of minced parsley, minced chives, minced capers, minced olives, minced cucumber pickle, and one teaspoonful of lemon juice. Blend thoroughly. Excellent for cold meats or fish.

French Dressing—This is the simplest of all dressings. Use an empty mayonnaise jar, or any jar with a tight top. Pour into the jar one cupful of olive oil and one-third cupful of lemon juice. Add one-third teaspoonful of salt, one-quarter teaspoonful of dry mustard, one-half teaspoonful of brown sugar and a dash of cayenne pepper. Drop a clove of garlic, cut in half, into the jar. Cover securely and shake well. There is no easier way to make French dressing. It will keep indefinitely, so it is wise to make it in large quantities. If it is to be kept, remove the garlic from the jar after it has stood fifteen minutes. Lemon juice is much better than vinegar, and infinitely more healthful.

Sour Cream Dressing—Beat one cupful of sour cream until stiff. Add three tablespoonfuls of lemon juice, one teaspoonful of brown sugar, one teaspoonful of salt, one-eighth teaspoonful of dry mustard and a dash of cayenne pepper. Beat all together. Add a few celery seeds, and one canned pimento, drained and chopped fine. This is an excellent sauce for cold slaw, cucumbers, cold ham or tongue.

Mock Mayonnaise—This is more economical than mayonnaise, and lends variety to the sandwiches. Melt one tablespoonful of butter in a saucepan. Add three tablespoonfuls of flour and blend. When the paste is smooth, add one cupful of boiling water. Stir and cook until a fairly thick white sauce results. Add two teaspoonfuls of salt, an equal amount of sugar, a dash of cayenne pepper, one-quarter teaspoonful of dry mustard. Blend thoroughly and remove from fire. Beat until very light the yolks of two eggs, add one cupful of olive oil, or any salad oil. Add four tablespoonfuls of lemon juice. Finally, pour in the hot sauce, beating constantly. Continue to beat vigorously for five minutes. Chill before using. This dressing can be used any time in place of mayonnaise. Tartare sauce, Russian dressing, or any of the fancy mayonnaises can be made with this as a base.

Russian Dressing—This is nothing but mayonnaise and Chili sauce. To one cupful of mayonnaise and one-half cupful of Chili sauce, add one tablespoonful each of chopped green pepper and chopped chives.

Cream Salad Dressing—To one cup of cream, whipped, add two tablespoonfuls of lemon juice, salt and cayenne to taste. Blend thoroughly and chill. This dressing cannot stand long. Sour cream may be used, with less lemon juice. This is excellent for nut sandwiches.

Condensed Milk Dressing—Make a smooth paste of one tablespoonful of mustard, one of

salt and a dash of cayenne pepper and a small
amount of lemon juice. Stir in one-quarter cupful of olive oil, or any salad oil. Add a scant
cupful of lemon juice. Beat well. Add three
well-beaten eggs and one fourteen-ounce can of
condensed milk. Beat for two minutes with egg
beater. Chill before serving. This will keep as
well as mayonnaise.

Cooked Salad Dressing—Many housewives
complain that cooked dressing is apt to curdle
in the process of making. If this recipe is fol-
lowed faithfully, it cannot curdle. Mix together
in a double boiler one teaspoonful of dry mustard, an equal amount of salt, one tablespoonful of brown sugar, one and one-half tablespoonfuls of flour and a dash of cayenne pepper. Add
two tablespoonfuls of olive oil, salad oil, or
melted butter. Blend to a paste. Add two well-
beaten egg yolks and one cupful of milk. Cook,
without allowing to boil, for seven or eight minutes. Stir constantly and do not allow the
dressing to stick to the bottom of the pan. Remove from the fire and allow to cool. When
cool add one-quarter cupful of lemon juice. Chill
before using.

Sweet Salad Dressing—Heat in a double boiler
one-quarter cupful each of lemon juice, orange
juice and pineapple juice. Beat two eggs until
light and add one-half cupful of sugar. Blend
together and add to hot liquid. Cook without
boiling until mixture thickens. About three
minutes is sufficient. Set upper half of double
boiler in cold water and beat until cold, adding
two tablespoonfuls of olive oil or salad oil. Just
before serving add one-half cupful of fresh or

sour cream, beaten. This is excellent for fruit salads, or for sweet sandwiches.

Hollandaise Sauce—This sauce may be used in place of mayonnaise, or to give the effect of a cream sauce in sandwiches. It is another sauce which is apt to curdle if proper care is not taken in preparing. Always use a double boiler. In the upper half of the boiler cream one-half cupful of butter until it is practically melted. Add the yolks of two eggs, one at a time, beating them well into the butter. When the mixture is smooth and well blended, add one-fourth teaspoonful of salt, a dash of cayenne pepper and one-half cupful of boiling water. Mix and cook until the mixture thickens. Stir constantly, allowing none of the mixture to stick to the bottom of the pan. When thickened, remove from fire and pour in the juice of one-half lemon. Beat. Allow to cool for sandwiches. Never try to reheat this sauce, as it will surely separate if you do.

Yellow Sauce—Make a medium thick white sauce, using soup stock if possible. Beat two eggs thoroughly and pour one cupful of the hot sauce over them, beating well. Add one tablespoonful of cream, beat, and add one teaspoonful of lemon juice. For sandwiches, cool before using.

Simple Hollandaise Sauce—Cream one-half cupful of butter in the top of a double boiler. Beat one egg, yolk and white, and stir into butter. Add one-half teaspoonful of salt, two teaspoonfuls of dry mustard, four teaspoonfuls of brown sugar, and a dash of cayenne pepper. Beat well, and cook in double boiler, adding

one-quarter cupful of lemon juice while cooking
When thickened, remove from fire. Chill for
sandwiches.

These three sauces are excellent for cold
meat or fish sandwiches. They give the effect
of a creamed meat, and also add variety.

In every case where lemon juice is required,
vinegar or half vinegar and half lemon juice
may be used. It is always best to use the
lemon juice, however, as vinegar is most dele-
terious to health. Besides, lemon juice gives a
much better and less astringent flavor,

VIII

THE BOX MEAL

There was a time when the only need for a
box meal was when a picnic was planned. Today, in rural communities at least, the picnic
is still in high favor. But there are other times
when a box lunch is desirable. The automobile
has instituted a new method of travel. Now,
the summer months see annual parade of mo-
tor tourists, winding slimly throughout the
country. It is an easy, delightful and, when
two or more are traveling, a most inexpensive
way of seeing the world. Inexpensive if done
properly, we should say. It is not economical
if the tourists stop at fashionable hotels every
night, or eat their meals in expensive restaurants. The actual camping grounds have been
set aside by a number of states. Here all the
necessary service is offered for a very small
sum. Only meals are not available. Here is

where the box meals come into their own. Delightful meals may be prepared cheaply if one starts with the proper equipment.

For touring, there are any number of cooking and serving kits. If one is going in for this sort of thing, one of these equipments is essential. Vacuum containers for food as well as beverages are now obtainable. Starting with these, almost anything is possible with little effort.

The box lunch has other uses, also. Many mothers prefer to send their children to school with their lunches, where it is impossible to have them come home, rather than let them buy anything in nearby lunch rooms. It is better for their health and much cheaper. Girls working in offices or shops have adopted the habit of carrying lunches. They can get better food, and have for recreation the time wasted in waiting for service in a crowded restaurant. Many working men carry lunches, also.

The demands on the box lunch are growing daily. How then can this meal be made as wholesome and appetizing as a meal at home? Ninety percent of such lunches that are carried today consist of sandwiches. And to say that ninety percent of those sandwiches are cold ham, cold roast beef, cheese or jelly is perhaps conservative. Sandwiches pack easily, is the usual excuse. Yes, and so do other things, if the proper container is used. Salads, vegetables, meats can all be carried, if the lunch box is adequate.

If the lunch is carried every day, the initial

expense of purchasing a proper box is well worth while. Only a light metal container should be used. The best boxes are arranged in compartments for the protection of the various foods to be placed in them. Vacuum boxes are obtainable now. Such containers will keep food hot or cold, in the same way that the vacuum bottles keep liquids at any desired temperature. The best lunch boxes contain a vacuum bottle for beverages. Such a box is essential for anyone who makes a habit of carrying his or her lunch.

If such a box is not obtainable, a very adequate substitute may be made at home. A fairly large tin cracker box will serve nicely. Have handy two or three small empty jars, with close fitting tops, which will fit into the box. With this simple equipment tasty wholesome lunches may be packed for the business girl, the school child or the working man. Such a box will also serve for picnics, although, in general, a much larger container is required for such festivities than is needed for a lunch for one person.

The main thing to remember is not to carry too much. As far as possible eliminate too many sweets, fat foods, and too much bread. Pie and layer cake is not usually satisfactory, unless the container is so arranged that these things may be packed without fear of squashing. The important thing is to choose such foods as will stand keeping, and to pack them in such a way that the lunch will look just as appetizing and fresh when the box is opened as it did when it was packed.

The menus suggested in the following chapters, except the final one, are only for one person. Any one of them may be expanded to serve any number of persons for a picnic or any other out-of-door function where a meal is required. These menus are arranged primarily for school children and working people.

IX

COLD BOX LUNCHES

Lunches for School Children Under High School Age

Children should eat simple food, and they should have something warm to drink, such as clear soup or cocoa, especially during the winter months. Make very simple sandwiches, using whole wheat, rye or Boston brown bread, and very little dressing. Never pack crackers in a lunch box. It is impossible to keep them crisp.

Clear Beef Soup
Alligator Pear Sandwich
Water Cress Sandwich
Manioca Jelly

Manioca Jelly—Manioca may be obtained at any large grocery store. It is more healthful than tapioca. Soak three dessert spoonfuls of manioca in cold water for six hours. Let it simmer in the same water with a bit of lemon peel until it becomes clear. Add any fruit flavoring, sugar to taste and a pinch of salt. Chill.

This may be kept for several days. Pack in a small wide-topped jar with a close-fitting lid.

2
Milk
Ham and Egg Sandwich
Dates and Cream Cheese
Sandwich
Apple Salad

3
Mutton Broth
Parker House Roll
Sandwich
Mixed Vegetable Salad

Pack the salad in a wide-topped jar with a close fitting lid.

4
Cocoa
Ham and Cottage Cheese
Sandwich
Sliced Tomatoes
Cold Slaw
Pound Cake

5
Chicken Broth
Whitstable Sandwich
Cuban Folds
Figs

Follow directions for Ham and Cheese sandwich, substituting cream or cottage cheese for the Swiss cheese, and omitting the Tartare Sauce.

6
Cream of Spinach Soup
Chicken and Tongue
Sandwich
Nut Dreams
Orange

7
Clear Vegetable Soup
Celery Sandwich
Stuffed Eggs
Sponge Cake

In making cream soups for box lunches follow the usual directions and make the soup slightly thinner. Clear vegetable soup can be made by mashing the vegetables through a sieve after the soup is cooked.

Stuff the eggs with any simple thing such as chopped ham, or tongue or chopped parsley and green peppers.

8
Milk
Salmon and Celery Salad
Boston Brown Bread,
Cream Cheese Sandwich
Apple

9
Cocoa
Waldorf Salad
Tongue and Chestnut
Sandwich
Manioca Pudding

Manioca Pudding—Mix three tablespoonfuls of manioca in one pint of milk. Cook over medium fire until it thickens or boils Remove from fire and pour into a bowl. Add one pint of cold milk, two well-beaten eggs and sugar to taste. Flavor with any fruit juice. Chill. This may be packed in small jars similar to those used for salads.

10
Beef Broth
Egg, Celery, Onion
Sandwich
Orange and Cream
Cheese Sandwich
Banana

11
Cream of Celery Soup
Mixed Fruit Salad
Chicken and Deviled
Ham Sandwich

12
Mutton Broth
Alligator Pear Salad
Apple and Bacon
Sandwich
Figs

13
Cream of Tomato Soup
Ham and Roast Beef
Sandwich
Apple

Alligator pears are one of the most healthful foods we can eat. To prepare for a box lunch, peel the pear, cut in thin strips or dice it, and mix with a small amount of French Dressing. Pack as other salads.

Roast beef for sandwiches should be fairly well cooked. All the fat and gristle should be removed.

14
Milk
Beet Salad
Tuna Fish and Cottage
Cheese Sandwich
Pound Cake

15
Beef Broth
Plain Hard-Cooked Eggs
Sliced Tomatoes
Banana Sandwich

Beet Salad—Dice cold cooked beets and mix with a small amount of chopped celery and cold fresh peas. Mix with a little sour cream dressing and pack.

Pack the eggs with the shells on. Slice the tomatoes and cover with a small amount of French Dressing or Mayonnaise, or pack them plain. Put salt in a separate container.

16
Mutton Broth
Cold Slaw
Mixed Unsalted Nuts
Bread and Butter

17
Milk
Tuna Fish Salad
Rye Bread and Cream
Cheese Sandwich
Raisins

Make the cold slaw with sour cream dressing. Sour cream is wholesome, and this dressing is better for children than mayonnaise.

Two ounces, or one-eighth of a pound of nuts is sufficient. Nuts are very healthful.

18
Split Pea Soup
Apple and Celery Salad
Tongue Sandwich
Dates

19
Lentil Soup
Fresh Vegetable Salad
Salmon, Onion, Celery Sandwich
Sponge Cake Sandwich

Make the soups in the usual way, but be sure they are thin enough to pour easily.

Of course the argument against this type of lunch for children is that they require the packing of knives and spoons. If the children have to bring home a lunch box, there is no reason why they cannot bring home the silver. In the matter of soup, if preferred, the soup can be taken from the small cup that covers every vacuum bottle. If the children are apt to lose the silver, cheap things can be bought in any Five-and-Ten Cent store. It is better to do this than to let the children eat improper meals.

LUNCHES FOR OFFICE WORKERS

There are also good lunches for high school children. Persons engaged in office work or other indoor, or sedentary work, should not eat heavy mid-day meals. No one should, but least of all these persons. Heavy food in the middle of the day makes the mind lethargic. Many persons complain that after lunch they want to lie down and sleep. This is because they have eaten too much. A light meal is better for the digestion, and infinitely better for the work to be accomplished. Nor should too much bread be eaten. It is just as easy to prepare and pack light salads as it is to make sandwiches. Such sandwiches as are used should be light, and should contain little or no meat. It is not so essential for grown persons to have a hot drink at noon as it is for children. Tea, coffee, milk, or any beverage preferred, or clear soup may be added to any of the following lunches, where none is specified.

1	2
Smoked Salmon Sandwich	Fresh Vegetable Salad
Hearts of Palm Salad	Egg, Crab Meat Sandwich
Dates	Banana

Drain the Hearts of Palm and cut in small pieces. Marinate for fifteen minutes in French dressing. Pack in a proper container with a small amount of French dressing.

3	4
Chicken Broth	Stuffed Eggs
Waldorf Salad	Smoked Salmon, Cold
Water Cress Sandwich	Slaw Sandwich
	Figs

The eggs may be stuffed with any favorite

filling.   Chopped parsley, onion, celery, green
pepper mixed with the yolks makes a delicious
stuffing.   It is better to avoid using meat fillings.

5	6
Chinese Vegetable Salad	Apple, Grapefruit Salad
Tuna Fish, Swiss Cheese	Date, Cream Cheese
Sandwich	Sandwich
Mixed Nuts	Banana

Chinese Vegetable Salad—These vegetables
may be purchased in cans from any large grocery store, or from the mail order houses.
They are delicious and healthful.   Drain bean
sprouts and water chestnuts.   Cut the latter
in small slices.   Mix together with a small
amount of French dressing.

The apple salad is made with equal parts of
chopped apple and chopped grapefruit.   A bit
of celery may be added.   French dressing with
a small amount of Roquefort cheese added
gives a piquant touch.

7	8
Beef Broth	Cold Pork Salad
Tartare Sandwich	Orange, Cream Cheese
Mixed Nuts	Sandwich

For the salad use left-over cold roast pork.
Mix with celery and chopped apple with a bit
of chopped onion.   Cover with mayonnaise or
sour cream dressing.

9	11
Alligator Pear Salad	Apple, Celery Salad
Roquefort Cheese	Ham and Egg Sandwich
Sandwich	Dates
10	12
Beet Salad	Shrimp Salad
Salmon, Onion, Celery	Swiss Cheese Sandwich
Sandwich	Sponge Cake

Make the shrimp salad more unusual by using sour cream dressing instead of mayonnaise.

13	14
Tomato, Cucumber Salad	Clear Vegetable Soup
Whitstable Sandwich	Apple and Bacon
Mixed Nuts	Sandwich

Chop equal portions of tomato and cucumber and drain for a few minutes. Add any seasoning desired and mix with French dressing.

15	16
Chicken Salad	Spinach, Ham Salad
Tomato, Horse-radish	Olive, Nut Sandwich
Sandwich	Raisins
Figs	

Spinach, Ham Salad—Be sure the spinach is well drained. To one cupful of minced spinach add one-half cupful of minced cooked ham, one tablespoonful of minced onion. Season to taste, and mix with a small amount of French dressing or mayonnaise.

17	18
Parker House Roll	Mutton Broth
Sandwich	Egg, Anchovy Sandwich
Mixed Nuts	Figs

A novel light filling for the Parker House rolls is cold slaw mixed with chopped onions and cucumbers. Use sour cream dressing.

19	20
	Asparagus, Hollandaise
Salmon Salad	Sauce
Sponge Cake Sandwich	Mock Crab Sandwich
	Dates

Drain canned or fresh cooked asparagus

well. Cut in convenient sized pieces. Cover
with cold Hollandaise sauce and pack.

21

Fruit Salad
Egg, Celery, Onion
Sandwich
Mixed Nuts

22

Chestnut Salad
Olivettes
Figs

Canned fruit may be used for the salad if
fresh fruit is not available. Fruits already
mixed for salad come in cans. If canned fruit
is used, drain for at least fifteen minutes before mixing with dressing. Any of the sweet
dressings may be used, if preferred.

Chestnut Salad—To one cupful of cold boiled
chopped chestnuts add one teaspoonful of
minced onion, an equal amount of minced
parsley and salt and pepper to taste. Mix
with French dressing or sour cream dressing.

23

Chicken Broth
Miami Sandwiches
Banana

24

Cream of Chestnut Soup
Favorite Sandwiches

Cream of Chestnut Soup—Cook the chestnuts
in a small amount of water until tender. Press
through a sieve. For every cupful of chestnut
pulp add one-half cupful of clear stock and
one half-cupful of rich milk or cream. Season
to taste. If preferred, all milk may be used
instead of the stock. If this is done, put a
stalk of celery, a sprig of parsley, and one
small onion in the water with the chestnuts
while they are cooking. Drain the chestnuts
and press through a sieve and return to the
water they were boiled in, adding as much

milk or cream as is necessary to make a thin cream soup.

25	26
Hearts of Palm Salad	Vegetable Salad
Egg, Ripe Olive Sandwich	Alligator Pear Sandwich
	Banana Sandwich
Dates	

Vary the hearts of palm salad by using yellow sauce or Hollandaise sauce in place of French dressing.

27	28
Stuffed Celery	Spinach, Cottage Cheese
Cuban Folds	Salad
Mixed Nuts	Nut Dreams
	Figs

Stuffed Celery—Use the small central stalks. Cut off the leaf ends, and wash and dry. Allow one scant tablespoonful of filling for each stalk. Mix equal parts of minced water cress, onion and the small yellow leaves of the celery. Season and make into a paste with mayonnaise. Fill the celery ends. By placing too of the stalks together, with the stuffed sides facing, these may be packed by simply wrapping in waxed paper.

Spinach, Cottage Cheese Salad—To one cupful of well drained, minced spinach and one teaspoonful of minced onion, an equal amount of minced parsley, and one-half cupful of cottage cheese. Blend together and mix with French dressing. This recipe is sufficient to serve two persons.

LUNCHES FOR WORKING PEOPLE

Men doing out-of-door work require a trifle more food than those working in offices. The general conception that a bulky sandwich or hunks of bread is a large amount of nourishment is false. Bulky does not mean nourishing. There is more actual food value in a small handful of nuts than there is in a hunk of bread, thickly buttered and slabbed with cold greasy meat. Such haphazard assortments of food only tend to disgust the appetite rather than awakening it. Sandwiches can be of the "man-sized" variety and still be dainty. Nor is there any reason why the out-of-door worker should not carry a small salad as well as the office worker. Again, in general, the matter of beverages will be left to the individual preference.

It is always best to make sandwiches of rye bread for packing. In general, rye bread does not get soggy as quickly as white or whole wheat bread does.

1	3
Apple, Celery Salad	Chopped Endive Salad
Combination Meat	Alligator Pear, Meat
Sandwich	Sandwich
Orange	Apple
2	**4**
Vegetable Salad	Chinese Vegetable Salad
Salami Sandwich	Ham and Egg Sandwich
Figs	Dates

To make the salad, wash and cut the endive into small pieces. Season with chopped onion, minced, parsley, and mix with French Dressing.

5	6
Chestnut Salad	Beet Salad
Pickled Pigs' Feet, Cold	Mock Club Sandwich
Slaw Sandwich	Dates
Orange	

7
Apple, Grape Fruit Salad
Tuna, Fish, Swiss Cheese
Sandwich
Raisins

8
Fruit Salad
Tongue, Chestnut
Sandwich

9
Alligator Pear Salad
Roast Beef, Horseradish
Sandwich
Figs

10
Tomato, Cucumber Salad
Salami, Onion Sandwich
Banana

11
Spinach, Cottage Cheese
Salad
Liverwurst Sandwich
Ripe Olives

12
Cauliflower Salad
Pork, Apple Sandwich
Dates

Cauliflower Salad—Use cold cooked cauliflower. Break the head into large pieces. To one cupful of broken cauliflower add one teaspoonful of minced onion, an equal amount of minced water cress, and a bit of chopped green pepper. Mix with French dressing or yellow sauce.

13
Okra Salad
Calf's Liver, Bacon,
Onion Sandwich
Apple

14
Asparagus, Hollandaise
Sauce
Salmon, Onion, Celery
Sandwich
Dates

Okra Salad—Boil and drain the okra. Cut in large pieces. Flavor with a small amount of minced parsley. Mix with Russian dressing, or French dressing. If the latter is used, a small amount of chopped tomato should be added to the okra.

15
Celeriac Salad
Corned Beef, Cold Slaw
Sandwich
Figs

16
Radish Salad
Cheese and Ham
Sandwich
Banana

Celeriac Salad—Celeriac is more commonly known as celery root. For salad use cold cooked root. To one cupful of the diced root add one teaspoonful each of minced onion, minced green pepper, minced parsley. Mix with French Dressing.

Radish Salad—Peel and slice the radishes. To one cupful add one teaspoonful of chopped chives, an equal amount of chopped parsley and two slices of cucumber diced. Mix with sour cream dressing or French dressing.

It must be remembered that when salads are prepared for box lunches, no lettuce can be used.

The recipes for all of the sandwiches will be found in the first part of the book. Other recipes can be found in any standard cook book, except those provided here.

X

HOT BOX LUNCHES

As we have stated before, a vacuum lunch box is absolutely essential if one is to carry a hot lunch. Be sure that everything meant to be warm is very hot before packing. Never try to pack hot sandwiches, as the bread will become soggy and unpalatatble. Hot meat, hot vegetables, any creamed dish can be easily packed if the proper container is used. One of the advantages of having proper equipment for carrying a hot lunch is that in general sandwiches may be eliminated. Sandwiches are not only apt to grow monotonous as a daily diet, but they are not the most wholesome things to eat consistently, since they require too much bread. The less bread we eat, the better off we are.

Of course, the hot dishes prepared must be simple. Lunches, hot or cold, are usually prepared in the morning before the worker leaves home. The mother or wife has the breakfast to prepare as well as the lunch. Involved dishes are therefore out of the question. But there are many simple things that can be made largely from left-overs. A few suggestions follow which will give the general plan of what a hot lunch should be like.

1	2
Creole Rice	Baked Sweet Potato
Mixed Vegetable Salad	Asparagus, Hollandaise Sauce

Creole Rice—This dish may be made from left-over rice. If possible use wild rice, or natural brown rice. The sauce is the main thing. This recipe is for six persons. The sauce may be made and kept indefinitely. Or, if preferred the recipe may be diminished. Mix together one finely chopped green pepper, half a cupful of mixed parsley and water cress, chopped; one large onion, chopped; two stalks of celery, chopped; and one cupful of canned tomatoes or of concentrated tomato soup. Add three tablespoonfuls of butter and let simmer slowly for about fifteen minutes, or until the vegetables are tender. Pour part of this over the rice to be used and heat slowly until the rice is warmed.

Baked sweet potatoes are very easy. Use small ones and put them in the oven while the breakfast is being prepared. They will cook in twenty minutes in a hot oven.

The asparagus may be cold or hot. The Hollandaise sauce should be made the night before. Do not try to reheat it. Have the asparagus very hot before pouring the sauce over it.

3	4
Hamburger Steak, Onions	Corn Pudding
Carrots and Peas	Swiss Chard Salad
Apple	Figs

Hamburger steak can be packed easily. It is better not to cook the onions. Slice them and pour boiling water over them, and allow to stand for fifteen minutes. Then drain and place over the steak.

Imported Swiss chard can be purchased anywhere. It is like endive in that it will not wilt quickly. Use French Dressing.

Corn pudding, made the night before, and heated in the morning, is an excellent box lunch dish. Chestnut purée, Lentils à la Maître d'Hôtel, Creole chestnuts, scrambled eggs, any variety of thin soup, any creamed meat or fish can be packed. Any type of hot vegetable is also good. Baked apples, either cold or hot, can be used as a box lunch dish.

These suggestions are merely to show the housewife the sort of food that will stand for several hours and not lose by it. The recipes for these dishes are found in any good cook book, or in *Unusual Menus*. When purées and soups are used, they should be prepared the day before and reheated before packing.

XI

HOT MEALS FOR PICNICS AND TOURS

The same sort of vacuum boxes may be used for picnics as are suggested for box lunches for working people. If a large number of persons are going on the picnic, and proper traveling facilities are available, such as automobiles, the possibilities for unusual meals are almost limitless. We will first consider just the one day picnic.

Soups are always good. They can be made at home, and heated over the camp fire. Of course, everyone knows that meat may be broiled and potatoes roasted. Many egg dishes are good for a warm picnic lunch. Scrambled eggs, Spanish omelette, creamed eggs, eggs Beauregarde, hot stuffed eggs are all possible. Do not try to carry the eggs in the shell. For the first two suggestions. Beat up enough eggs before leaving home. Place them in a tightly covered jar, and cook them when you reach the picnic ground. For the others, have the eggs hard-cooked before starting. In the case of stuffed eggs, prepare them at home, all but the final heating. In a tightly covered jar place enough cold white sauce. Take along a small shallow pan. When ready for the dish, fix the eggs for cooking, cover with a lid and place on hot coals until warmed. The recipe will be found in *Unusual Menus*. Any creamed dish makes an excellent hot meal for a picnic. The cream sauce may be cooked at home and packed in a covered jar. The meat, fish, or whatever food is to be served, may be cut and seasoned and packed at home, then combined with its sauce, and heated over the picnic fire when the time comes to serve it.

The matter of camping or touring requires greater attention. Everyone who owns an automobile likes to tour during the summer months. It is an easy pleasant way to spend the family vacation. It can be very economical, also. The main thing is, not to overcrowd the car with useless baggage. A proper camping outfit may be obtained at a small cost and attached to the side or rear of the car. Such an outfit must contain enough dishes and knives, forks and spoons for service. A small hatchet for cutting wood, a can opener and a very sharp knife are essentials.

Do not try to carry enough staple foods to serve for the entire trip. In any village or town such commodities may be purchased. The wisest way is to carry just enough food for a day's meals. When leaving a town in the morning, buy supplies for the day. Or, if there is plenty of room in the car, certain staples may be carried to last several days. Coffee, tea, canned milk, sugar, salt, pepper, bread and canned soups are safe, easy things to carry.

Pots and pans are the great problem. Until you have tried it, you will be surprised how little is really necessary. For four persons the following cooking equipment is sufficient. One coffee pot, one medium sized frying pan and one or two medium sized sauce pans. That is all. The most delightful meals can be cooked with these things.

One of the everlasting problems of camping is greasy dishes, and pans. The easiest way to avoid these, is to omit greasy foods. Do not fry meats, broil them. They are more delicious this way, and leave less to clean up afterward. Long sharp clean sticks are excellent for broiling bacon. Run the stick through three or four strips of bacon and hold them over the flames, far enough away so that the bacon will not burn, until the meat is crisp. Chops, steaks, ham may be broiled without the use of a pan. Take along a toaster with long handles, or if possible, a square iron grating. The top of the broiler from the kitchen stove will serve, if nothing else is obtainable. Such a grating can be set up on sticks, high enough over the flames to avoid burning, and any sort of meat cooked on it. In this way, most of the grease drips into the fire, leaving only the light grating to be washed.

It is not wise to carry uncooked eggs in the shells. If they are to be scrambled or made into an omelette, break them into a jar before starting out in the morning. When ready for use, mix them and cook. Hard-cooked eggs may be prepared while the breakfast is cooking. Before making the camp fire, dig a shallow hole in the ground. Lay as many eggs as desired in the hole. Cover with leaves and a bit of earth. Make the fire on top of this nest. When you are ready to leave the place, brush away the fire remnants, remove the eggs, and pack away until needed. Of course, they will not cook as quickly as they will in boiling water. It requires about half an hour to hard-cook eggs by this method.

Do not depend entirely upon canned food. Such a diet spoils the trip. Stop at farm houses, or at the markets in the various towns, and buy a few fresh vegetables, for the evening meal at least. If you are cooking coffee or soup, it is wise to prepare enough for two meals. It can be poured into vacuum bottles and kept in excellent condition until needed. This saves time and trouble. Enough meat may be prepared at the evening meal to be served cold for the noon meal or the evening meal the following day.

Figs, dates, raisins and nuts are excellent things to carry for the whole trip. They keep indefinitely and are always good. Before starting on the trip but two or three pounds of mixed shelled nuts in an air-tight tin box. They will retain their crispness for several weeks, and will be very useful additions to the lunch menus. The dried fruits may be mixed together and put in another tin box. With these things handy, you always have something to fall back on for a meal, even provided that you pass through no towns or villages where other edibles may be obtained.

By using a little discretion, by not overloading your car when you start, your touring vacation may be made delightfully simple, and you will be independent of roadside restaurants and hotels.